Wild Animals on the Moon

& Other Poems

by

Naomi Ayala

CURBSTONE PRESS

Printed in the U.S. on acid-free paper by BookMobile
Cover design: Chris Thorkelson

Some of the poems in this manuscript have appeared in the following
periodicals: *Poetry USA*: "A Coquí in Nueva York"; *Kalliope*: "It Was Late
& She Was Climbing;" *The Caribbean Writer*: "A Man Will Rush from
Behind Me," "Amber Hands;" *Callaloo*: "Lawns" and "Wild Animals on the
Moon," "Immigrant's Voice," "Words," "Haiti," "For 'S'," "Airborne,"
"Fifteen-Ten," "For Late Nite Poems" and "Abuelo's Garden"; *In Creative
Resistance: U.S. Puerto Rican Women*: "Morela from Peru," "Dance,"
"Words"; *The Massachusetts Review*: "Papo Who'd Wanted to be an
Artist," and "Reform;" *Hip Magazine*: "A Mighty Servant Who Never
Sleeps."

This book was published with the support of the Connecticut
Commission on the Arts and the National Endowment for the
Arts.

Library of Congress Cataloging-in-Publication Data

Ayala, Naomi, 1964—
        Wild animals on the moon, and other poems / by Naomi Ayala.
    — 1st ed.
        p.   cm.
        ISBN 1-880684-44-6
        1. Title.
        PS3551.Y23W55   1997
        811'.54—dc21   96-45140

published by
CURBSTONE PRESS   321 Jackson Street   Willimantic, CT 06226
        phone: (860) 423-5110   e-mail: info@curbstone.org
                        http://www.curbstone.org

Contents

III.

IV.

This book is for my family,
especially youngest Gabriel—
as far as China, as high as the sky.

Acknowledgements

I am indebted to Hedgebrook Farm in Whidbey Island, WA for providing me the time, space and good food to work on my writing at the most important time of my development. An emergency grant from Change, Inc. made it possible for me to continue with my work during a time of great financial distress.

Lillian, Reynaldo and Milton Ayala made room for my words in the *huerto* of their lives and watered them regularly. Titi Carmen and Tío Manuel gave me my first home in the U.S. and kept me from going without. Carmen Delgado, Frank Caciutto, James Ramedei and Carol Grabowski spent countless hours teaching me English so that I could write poetry in that second language while Manuel Durán made sure I remained proficient as a writer in the first. I am equally grateful to *Casa Cultural Julia de Burgos,* New Haven's stubborn and courageous activist community, the troops at the Greater New Haven Arts Council, my students and the staff at Cooperative Arts & Humanities High School, Martín Espada and Jack Agüeros, without whom this book would not have been possible, Carl Legere, Campbell Dalglish, Jack Hirschman, Marianela Medrano, Laura Kelly Wagner, Stephanie Kelly and, by far not least, to my publishers, Alexander Taylor and Judith Doyle, for their longtime support and loving validations.

I.

Immigrant's Voice

I heard an immigrant's voice.
It rubbed the walls of downtown
buildings clean,
wiped the glass of steamy truckstop
windows with its breath
& o.d.'d on caffeine
& cigarettes , dawns before work.

It cleared a fog in January
with its whistle in its jeans,
climbed the flagless pole on the Green & shouted,
itself a mast recited
from the dollar
e pluribus unum e pluribus unum.

It prayed in front of the gates
of Union Trust,
climbed city hall steps — kneecaps to concrete
during unemployment —
& asked the mayor, please, a shot of whiskey
or dope, or a dollar, a mighty dollar.

It cut open its forearm six inches
at his machine operator's job
cutting steel —
his words deep-blue-purple
but he had to be grateful,
had to be grateful for the work.

It pounded on its lover's breast,
this voice
demanding *where* is the dream?
Where *is* the dream?

It broke into tears at public urinals
& spit on statues on the way home
until sweat poured
from the contour
of their histories.

It gargled the news
nights after suppertime
& crawled shivering into its sleep.
What sleep there could be.
What dreams.

The Tattoo

— for Reynaldo

The tattoo came after we'd moved
after the pale green LeMans
burned to pieces along the side
of the highway & we'd lost our brother
Max to bourbon & pot & dope & suicidal
acrobatics in the afterhours of dark rooms.

It was a dragon, cost a lot,
stung a lot. He had to work up
the guts for a long time.
I almost got one too,
a rose. He loved roses.

He wasn't the dragon sort at 16.
Every time he tried to spew fire
out came the roses.

But this was before Max,
before die-casting, the wife
that came with the child
and the child that came afterwards.

He wears a headwrapped bandana
with his shop uniform.
He can keep his hair long that way now.

I tell his wife about the roses,
how he gave one to every girl,
how his tattoo
could've been a long-stemmed rose
luminous and delicate as his eyes
& he keeps quiet,
very, very quiet when she laughs.

A Man Will Rush From Behind Me

Duerme mi pequeña.
No vale la pena despertar.
Voy a salir, por ahi, ahora,
trás la aurora más serena.
Duerme mi pequeña...

A man will rush from behind me,
slam my body to the ground until
blood flowers from my elbows.
Later, the obligatory slap to shut
out the scream.
He will take more
than my purse, thrash round places
softer than my womb.
Call me a white bitch.
Leaving his sweat on my body, whisper
how I deserve the pain.

I carry his memory in my ovaries.
They throb when I walk, want to scream
out in Spanish for the world
to leave me the hell alone.
I have been walking anyway —
stopping at corners to turn,
growl at the steps that quicken
behind me, ghost steps.

While the palm trees of Luquillo Beach
sing at the mouth of my stomach
until the song begins to bubble,
each note swirls up my esophagus
like bittersweet acid,
breaks from my tongue.
I want to think this will protect me,

make me less afraid;
there is a home sheltered inside of me,
not a home trapped inside the street.
I have been free before
and can remember it.

Once, I dreamt myself inside
the belly of a mountain
in the Cordillera Central,
just to test my freedom,
and it took me days to get out.

This is not a mountain
and I am awake.

Race

In your eyes I am not a woman.
You see me, my face square
as La Plaza de San Germán,
so square a place
you feel you can walk
through it any time you want
without taking the time to sit down,
feed the hungry
bastard pigeons of your solitude,
without whistling from inside our humanness,
and you might be thinking
I don't belong
any place anymore than you do,
so you push me around
thinking you are pushing yourself around
but I belong. I am whole,
wholesome, every drop of sun
inside my fruit.

Despite you
I celebrate my clay-softening hands,
my island-country song full of flowering
compost heaps where there should be graves.

Yes, me.
I praise the power behind my song
and my singing, behind where I've been
and know I will be going.

You might say I'm crazy
singing like I do,
but my love is green, wild
fields of *morivivi*,
beside you.

El Yunque

Across from Luquillo Beach,
a house without walls,
womb of moist, rich earth
where I am thirteen
and my tiny breasts howl
at dawn, light falls
from the trees like nectar, the wind
the strum of a cuatro
whose *jíbaro* soul swoops
to knock songs from my mouth —
songs that will learn
to swim up the river.
In that place
where the stones talk back,
low clouds carry aphrodisiacs,
wild flowers leave
the poems of their scent
on my thighs. Plump words rain
onto corrugated zinc roofs
with the sharp tongue
of hunger lashing at invisible clocks.
The slow rhythms of the earth
can be pulled up
with the gait of the feet.
I know this house
like the back of my sleep.
I dance there everyday, a winged-woman,
no matter how far I might travel.

Abuelo's Garden

He pointed to tomatoes
we harvested in our backyard
and called them tiny worlds,
took a swig from his *caneca*
pretending to be
pentecostal still.
I was 12, believer
of island-planets
in a future garden.
How they should hang
like tomatoes from their stems,
grow plump alone together.

Fifteen-Ten

As the native Taíno population dwindled
in 1510, the first African slaves were brought
by the Spaniards to the island of Borikén.

you came to us a young woman
made to couple out back by the pens
with your brother
while guards peered laughing,
determined
whether you did it the same way
as they'd trained us to.
still they took you
themselves just to make sure,
made your brother an ox,
chained him to a pole to sleep standing
while more of you were dragged
face down in the dirt
and we, all of us
dying one limb at a time.
today i remember you first,
your strong eye
meeting mine across a field.
you, beaten by rape into a hard wood
a song burning room in you
for the child of pain
in my home, sister
where it was supposed to be safe,
where it was supposed to be love
meeting you, love.

Queen Joy

You were lean mean in your caramel
sweetness, lean mean honeypie
could scope
malefiction with the wide
eye of your confident
neighborhood self
smelled faraway laughter like leftover
food in the supermarket
of your garbage cans.
Good Lord, Queen Joy
what did the streets
do with you? How far
did they swallow you down
with your cart of pots
for your stone soup dreams
your chains, books, radio
your super-duper rescue bags
of imaginary provisions and noontime tea?
Good Lord, Queen Joy
what will we do when our death
comes to us without a photograph
of you, your holiday date
of neighborhood history, without
something like your tattered
black hat to hold to our breasts?
Good Lord, Queen Joy
the streets are meaner everyday,
have built trickdoors downtown.
We sleep with clubs and rattles
at our feet. You can't even trust
the corner to be good to you, to deliver
a napkin for your tears.

Even at the March

Even at the march this year
thousands of Boricuas gathered in D.C.
on stage left, the American flag
on stage right, the Puerto Rican.
A friend, who was there
who also reads from left to right
like all gathered read
like television cameras pan
left to right this evening
took notice, unfurled a comunique.
Who else could see? Me, a thousand
gathered into me. America,
you're always trying to ride me.
Ride me on my back.
Ride me with my own even.
I sleep with one eye open
the other scopes the spirit world
for signs—retreat, come forward
retreat, come forward, explode
take back my face; a strategy
for the sum of all parts—
and this one that is me
island-home, my country.
Its fertile land to return
mended spirit-earth
failed promises to vanish.
And, a flag like a name
I must be called rightly
amast at all the hills
of our gathering... waiting in line
not waiting, out the window
by the grocery store
at the airport where I try
to forget this coming and going
has a name I belong to.

Glass

— for Gayle Hall, activist, poet,
single parent of seven and adoptive mother of one.

I am a woman learning to be free
Every day I weep
drawing chipped glass
from my calloused feet

Papi said vases can be glued & bowls & figurines
when I was small
My brother says *now, ain't no use holding*
            on to broken things
My lover says *let me give you kisses*

My history is glass I walk on
 with my soul on fire
I am a woman learning to be free
My history pours hard over my shoulders
 blows like a typhoon

and I become thunder in the dark
and my eyes tell no lies
they say *free me* when I talk every day

I weep drawing chipped glass
from my calloused feet
gathering all the pieces afterwards

Words

Through the coffeeshop mob
out by the rose stand
the streetlamp beams on gold tooth word
& sweaty brow
on delicate, fur-lined neck
words slipped up in cold air
on the silk word
& ringed-hand flutter.
Words never went half-price here.

Window shopping through the stone fort
walls of Yale University
in consignment words too tight
here, too loose there
but past the inspection points
of the private library, prepared
for the secret feast, sly word kleptomaniac:
caught, run out & known by sight now.

A mile past the smoke stack & tracks
words writhe on brown bodies
faint print housedresses metaphorize
warm words soothe with their ashen
working hands, sweet words
dunked in strong coffee & bitter words
passed like a half-pint at a funeral.

I salute those, unpurchasable they leap
& soar from mouths with what true
dignity there is, search out each other
&, in between the daily stumbling, push
firmly toward a center where they all meet.

In a World of Few Merengues

— for Elizabeth Ortiz

When the bars close
& there ain't nobody to keep everybody's eyes
lit under the world.
When the street is unsafe
and the house is unsafe,
she is ahumming a mouth-to-soul resuscitation.
The music never stops inside.
She sweeps with her dance.
Her dance is in her sweeping.
   Breaking bread between the broken
smiles of deprivation
and the vena cava of her music mind,
she feeds all of herself.
The world is in her body.

II.

The Night I Walk Into Town

The night I walk into town
to meet my brother
I'm tripped up
by a car whose wheels rip
through a newspaper
along the white line
of the road.
The black bold
type is bleeding.
I scream
but the bleeding doesn't stop.
At the corner a man who hasn't seen
water, food, gloved fingers
this cold, snow-blowing January
asks how many faces do I see
holding his chin up.
Twenty-five, I say
twenty-five thousand.

If We Passed You

be calm. don't worry. no one
will trade your hands
for theirs. no fingers
to be lost, empty sockets
to bleed a hollow weep
for anything.
lock the door of your car.
alarm the house.
no one will come
to get you.
thieves only want the purse,
t.v., car stereo
not your children, silence, vote
for anything.
life need not be a security bond
to move a mob a little forward.
know, know where you're going
and you won't be lost.
nothing be lost.
no one change the channel
on you, drop a bomb on your house
cut out your tongue
for speaking in private too often,
making change,
a favor,
keeping your loyalties,
having friends.
no one will come to get you
for anything.
child molesters are not organized,
cartels and serial murderers
haven't got a political purpose.
you can move away from crime
smell of rare perfume
while small suns glisten
on your breast. why worry so

while you dance in your fine
underwear, shirts,
skirts, pants that feed people?
you are food.
others be thankful for your labor,
your food
through dreamy hollywood sweatshop
coffeebreaks abroad.
of course you believe in liberation.
everyone be liberated like you,
be food,
have lawns,
a Guatemalan, Colombian, Puerto Rican,
Cuban, Dominican, Haitian woman
of 50 to keep house,
a carpenter to add new wings
when you wish, wake up, feel like it
to store objects of your choice, taste,
taster's choice:

the unseen flesh of hands, fingers
buried in your ceramic pots,
pots glazed with blood
so perfectly positioned
on your display pedestals.
the serigraph of woman selling child
on a street for food
skillfully hung
by you in the room for living.
your husband's van heusen shirt collar
and the stain of the maquilladora's rape
over it that you managed
to erase so well with clorox.

the objects of your taste
will outlive
you passing hands, being traded,
collecting shades of light

19

and dust elsewhere in your absence
and you dead, dispensably dead,
having left no trace of your own breath
been so easily replaced
by thousands.

if we passed you and forgot to scream,
forgive us.

What Am I?

What am I
in White
america?
A word
mis-
pronounced & beaten
down
each
time
by a
different
new
name.
A name
out
of any
kind of un-
union.
The tender marrow
inside my bones
remembers so many
names back.
You who make me
a tenement
language
inside your white
walls,
invent for me
a new
word to mean "be"—
the being
you want to push
me to become.
A word you
can use
like a marble

spinning
on the wheel
of your world's roulette.
So praise
being! I am myself
outside your words.
Praise any new word.
You will always
have to call me something.

Poverty

It gives you pigeon eyes,
makes you brave
as a cracked slate
with all the weight
of a house on top.

It bids you
hold out your quaky hand
through bittersweet temptations.

You dream of it as slick
silvery fish between your hands
wide eyed & breathless
but it circles your bleeding
feet like sharks.

At evening time
between lampposts & garbage
drums turned over in the wind,
poverty is black ice...
or a train, whose departure you miss,
whistling at you in the distance.

Your will is chalky on your tongue
like aspirin
& patience hangs like frayed
dreads down your back.

Morning bends
the scalpel-sharp pain
in the rib cage,
love's sulfur-dazed eyes.

Two tea bags in your wallet
for when the day is done
& poverty at your feet

like a hungry dog
laps up the sweat of your calves.
You come & go not speaking
fumbling for a ripcord
through a thousand leagues of wild wind.

A Mighty Servant Who Never Sleeps

Summer heat
without air

the loud thunder
of machines
cutting steel

They live two blocks
from the plant
Jorge's tired
            siempre
Dad's in pain
            siempre
Jorge can't speak
English and people
            are afraid
because he might be
 Cuban-communist
Milagros is afraid
because
her children are

Her home is reckless
but the Lord
is with her
When she does
the dishes
he's there
she's been pregnant
every year
for the past six
The pastor
does not believe
in birth control
and Jorge is waiting
for them to wait

for the children
to wait
so is Milagros

When the steel
industry
was doing well
our family
was gasping
in the Hill
Fair Haven
Newhallville:
the plant's
waste disposal
for those
life-sentenced
to machines
who weren't
allowed to mediate
            delegate
the bullshit
handed over to them

Still dad got
every order
out on time
on Sunday
before Christmas
before breakfast
doubleovertime
I despised
his dedication

When the steel
industry
was doing badly
it broke his back
before the plant

closed down
years tattooed
with scars
insufferable
tendonitis
and we followed
as children do
       hating the move
       hating mother
       hating rice again for dinner

It's over for us now
       this is a thing
of the past
The Scar Awards Office
delivered its verdict
and the checks come
But Jorge's still waiting
       siempre
through doubleover time
with Milagros
two towns away
       from this one

Papo, Who'd Wanted to be an Artist

Papo, lying on a Divine Street bench,
the divinity of neighborhood
angels kissing open his eyes.
Hymns, hymns for the angels
to whose work-beaten faces cling
the fishing nets of insomnia between the broken
bottles of missed hits at the numbers
store and the traffic going by. Papo,
he has small brown hands
that reach out from his eyes.
With them he smears the pollen
of *amapola* memories, dreams up an entire
town of angels, faces the color of the sun.
Amidst this flowering, he calls
for Ochún, her tight embrace. Ochún,
who has been in hiding. Once,
during a great experiment of will,
Papo managed to pull silver
wings from Miguel's *costado* —
just before Miguel died. He had him flying
through smog, concrete, out to the air
bus he was always missing.
But Papo could not come along with him.
How was he to get back afterward?
Angels have such short life spans.
And, how was he to know?
That night, Ochún greeted him
with blood-red roses,
kissed his small weeping hands,
gave him moon
water from her breasts.
He was sure she'd come out this way again.
He had been waiting politely.

It Was Late & She Was Climbing

It was late & she was climbing
up the hill with her babies,
late and he climbing onto her —
her belly glowing fire.
She climbed the steps of the day
with all she could carry
& the day climbed onto her, too
& they rolled together until night broke
them into pieces they looked
for in the morning.
Everywhere light
spilled out from her belly.
It doubled with every touch.
This went on for a long time
until everything around her became light.
Late & no matter how early,
dawn sometimes,
she went on blinding birds
& men & children
& women showed up to her house wearing visors
& she had to hug every thing & everyone
to grow small enough
to fit into her climbing.

Airborne

Lower Dixwell, near April,
sallow as small hands
in the casket of a child
you last saw yesterday
playing trampoline on a mattress
by the corner store
in the eye of a pool
of broken glass.

Today midday rises like exhaust,
the pungent scent of flowers at a wake,
rides on the belly-smooth rooftops
of slow-moving cars

shouts out to you
to come closer and stop,
forget what
you could have come for.

Midday, embodied in the music
of cars that pass you
with windows rolled down in the rain,
beat thumping against fogged windshields
and spilling out onto the sidewalk,
base loud enough to
razor-graze your sadness.

In my arms a broken heap
of machine guns
cold as December
bears into my soft flesh.
Where *do* I set this down?
Already I carry the blood and sweat —
a metal taste on the tongue
you cannot wash.

At my feet are names
spelled with loose triggers,
empty shells, chalkmarks.
Tyronne. Luis. Tony Ocasio.

I am a woman saving names
in a soft-leather purse of silence.
Tony — Tony Ocasio —
who didn't like to be called Juan.

I could spit bullets
with the dry cough
that bolts me out of sleep.
Inside my eyes barrels
line the cornea
despite flowers in my throat
that once opened to love,
April mornings,
a man.

Where my arms freeze-burn
and bruise there will be callouses.
The flowers of my throat sleep
under a sheet of ice.

I am a woman
holding up the corner stop sign
with the bones of my back,
arms weighed down to my hips,
a woman calling out names.

Everyday

He could taste the end
of his last night.
— Gabriel Tadeo Ayala

The people who sell you jeans & tennis shoes,
from whom you buy the newspaper
to see your life outlined
in someone else's photograph
know your days are nomads
leaving their slash & burn
to burrow in your cells.
Soon there will only be lists — alphabetized,
in small print — to check against
the names of everyone you know
& death will be the shadow
you can't shake no matter how you dance
on hot coals to smelt the spirit,
how you run from it.
Of course mornings are insane,
the waking, though you are
grateful for the sun.
How could you not be?
You sing yourself into your day
through the clink & clatter of the city
dreaming of an underground to defect to
though this is your home,
home-country, occupied
by a brilliantly white death standing
militantly at each corner,
yelling for you to stay in,
keep the bounds of your curfewed life,
remember who you are.
But you know who you are everyday,
know the color
of the inside of your breath,
dance & sing & get up

everyday to meet it all over again.
Your soul is a spirit-gathering drum
for the defying hands of your laughter.
Your tongue a sea
-bird who can rhyme blue oceans
awake from their careful sleep.
You know strength comes
from everywhere nights like tonight,
nights that are bottomless,
days a young child wraps around your knee,
everybody's child,
asking *What do you see*
from up there? What do you see?

III.

Sixteen

                i wanted
the dream shampoo —
kinks in my hair, to tread
                their spongy
softness
with my fingertips.

                        i wanted
chocolate brown skin
for the man
i loved.
not to apologize,
explain
the vaina about my ancestry.

                not to have to say *yes.*
                                yes.
                                        yes.
Boricua? yes.
                        yes.
bothsides.
                not to have to say
watch me how i speak.
                watch
                me how
                i speak.
watch me how i dance
                a mean
                merengue.

El Placer de la Palabra

The pleasure of your speaking.
   The loud rivers
of your speaking. The soft, bending
   arch of recognition
between your smile & the speed of busy
hands at the salary of a cab,
bus, in the restaurant
   of our millionaire ambition
   minimum-waged into this narrow
   small-breathing dream
we call a golden country.
   Azúcar
negra. Brown sugar. *Te quiero*. I love
   your speaking. I go
   with loving rhythm
through the revolving
   door of days spent moving
   without moving. I find you & my ear
is a blackhole for the music
   of your dancing tongue.
My body is a blackhole.
   If I carry *home* on my back —
crawling into foxholes
into the safeway of night —
 when I pass you carrying all you have
on your own hardened back, your words
 bring the cool sweat to the heat
of my daily life. And, I stop
   to court you, *azúcar*
negra, brown sugar, your tongue
   to drink of your crystal
clear music.

Reform

You know we have always been poor,
always been suspect, the ragwater cocktail
of their bad dreams. And, Rebecca, again they say
they want us to be free. Fuck this, fuck that
stuff of salvation by handout assistance.
They want yet for us another freedom of *progress
in self-sufficiency* while they fingerprint
our hands for food. And, nobody's talking up
our case rationally enough, they say.
Yet these are the times of organized lunacy —
though no one fingerprints them for our tears.
No one fingerprints them for our hunger.
José, where could I be now? Ten miles east
of a hot plate of food? Frankie, what more
can they do? Bodyslam us where your body lay
in the street till we bleed again through you?
How to scratch the eyes out
of the face of hunger's monster, María,
when you're too weak to be clear, drowning
slow death by drowning in their filth?
Is it like cooking for eight children?
Half yours, half not your own?
Is it easier than not having enough?
Is it harder than the future?
How will we kick back out of this one?
Who will come for us, Miguel,
if we are too broken?
The sign of the cross here's
been waking gunshyless & believing
tomorrow might be the same
as we rub the rosary beads of employment
listings so they may yield.
Anything resembling walls will have to
suffice for a house. Even the coffin of our children's
time-bombed lives the moment they leave our wombs.
And praying's done me personally so much

good, now I bask in the luminosity
of neon, in his rainbow-colored song,
believe one day he too might come for me
like the god of employment — off his information superhighway
shortcut with the sanctity
of city dump angels beating
their aluminum wings.

I Have Not Asked You

Mother, I have not asked
how you splintered me off into the world.
If I lie beside you
now — a grown woman —
tears rushing,
hands in a quiver, it is
that the questions in you
renew themselves in me
over and over.
Once, as a child
you wrung from my limp body
infection, resurgent fever
unblinking, your body calm
& I could be blind
beside you, breathing more easily.
But how, I ask you, mother,
did your hands remain so soft,
did you keep the color
of your eyes through men
pushing you into walls.
Did you ever reach
for *abuela* in the dark,
reach and call to her
when the day pulled taut
the thin blue line of your life?

Dance

— for Lillian Ayala

Dance to Chopin's Nocturne
E minor, Opus 72,
kissing the aches
away from his leaves
of absence
leaving your lipstick
between the folds
of bedroom curtains
at the last crescendo
for your other lover to find

D a n c e prima
donna of keys to private places
and scarecrows in the back-
yard of the ages,
dance a guaracha
to the rumble of the fridge
s
  t
    r
     e
      t
       c
        h
the 9 to 5 off
achy feet
epsom salt
soak of the spirit
toes pointed
to tomorrow, arms
a lift of wings
to the mirror-music
of your secret radio

The Week I Was Eighteen

I left the week I was eighteen.
Mami made it to Puerto Rico
for vacation, through a front porch
of Salvation Army chairs, boxed things.
She said I would not leave —
simply, like "It will rain tomorrow."
Papi watched t.v. without moving,
hugging a beer can without drinking.
His eyes followed me when I was
not looking. He was in the living
room for days. Youngest Gabriel
was five that year. Lillian would soon
leave for college. Max, Reynaldo
pushed their boyhood into the smoky
glass of their lives. The telephone
barely rang. No one sent letters
from far off. I was not expected anywhere
at anytime. It was the summer of gypsy moths.
The summer of two hundred dollars
to last out a rent, food, the bus
to work, to last out the feeling
of being rich enough to climb
my own tree, smoke my own cigar,
walk backwards if I had to. Luck
had a lot to do with it. Though winters
came and went, long winters in my beautiful
America where dreams had no spine
to them and no, I'd not been concealing
a coming child. Life's muddy potholes rolled
into view, got me stuck in them, filled up
with the prickly grass of time, and no,
I'd not been living off of a man.
I used to think I was pretty spectacular.
Today I know I was looking
for love in secret places no one before
me thought to look, thought she would

43

be able to have to.
Today I think that somewhere
far beyond my imagination, a girl
will have my eyes and hands and feet
and someone who remembers me
will tell her about me.

Landscape

I.

Saturday. Failed sleep.
Clumsy trips across a house
for things I can't remember
I don't need. Your name,
a memory, leaps like a cat
in front of my feet & I'm already down
before I can look down. Between the cracks
of the floor boards is you,
you in the air, you out the window & I
waiting. Some good woman I am to leave
no room for me in my own house.

II.

Just last night in Pittsburgh,
climbing Mt. Washington on an incline,
I saw three rivers come together,
felt them meeting the way wind meets the skin.
　　　　An immense sky
where I could see myself
& breathe, remember to breathe, opened
all in one click over a track tie.
I felt myself intelligent
in my bones.
　　　　Present.
But you were there too,
later, late night
beside letters I could not write you,
inside things, like a good woman

45

I try to explain
over & over.
            How does a woman explain
a knot in the throat?
A tightening above the breasts?
Cold absence surging up the spine?
Gaps in love & words her feet get stuck in
to make her not move so
swiftly, freely, to impair
            her walking?
She does. She holds the knot in one hand
like blown glass. With the other
she does dishes & is quiet
on the outside, quiet
over the cooking pots & tells a child
not to worry & listens to a child & marathons
to her job, a second one or the third
& comes home to shower
& sleeps half-awake, all the while
holding that hand up,
            trying to explain.

III.

Today the afternoon fell over the length
of Orange & State Streets
            over my shoulders.
Somebody put it there, I thought.
I am not alone. I learn
to breathe more carefully now,
outside, today, as if
I were inside someplace trying
to calm myself down.
Inside a mall
minus the stores, walls, bags, loud letters,
bold money signs, with pockets empty of want,
            minus the oxygen
cramped up in front of me.
And I am invisibly ascending floors

without moving, minus the music,
just as desolate.
　　　My mind is quiet inside itself
from so much fear,
not from so much goodness.

IV.

Yes, this is about landscape.
About zigzagging in & out of places
where I can & cannot see myself.
About running, about being crazy
about distortions & about being distorted
into a backdrop of neon dreams.
I am not alone, really.
This is about landscape.
A face inside a face inside another.

V.

I wanted to walk out to Fair Haven today,
　　　past La Casa Green & slow salsa
pouring from the music store —
　　　slow like a slow breath —
over to El Coquí so I could walk
　　　with a *pastelillo* in my hand,
listen to the scattered trees who must
　　　be singing in the voice
of Willie Colón, Celia Cruz, Eddie Palmieri.
　　　They must be singing just for me
'cause I am not alone.
And, something's trying to tell me this
is about landscape. A face inside
a face inside another & a single
set of eyes looking out into the world.

VI.

America.
Too many people walked that air bridge
       for me too many times.
And, come to find me here a woman
beside a man I love,
walking on air, sweat-stained, bloody
       stolen air.
It is in my breath.
And my feet no longer have a place
to go to for too long
without you everywhere.
       My feet are growing old.
They know the wee hours of the morning,
wake me up hollering about you,
about this man I love,
       about air bridges that don't hold up
in the middle of the night.

VII.

       This
is about landscape.
About a face inside a face inside another,
about how, past waking,
sometimes you do not see me anymore
as if I were air
& I am a woman with a knot in my throat
trying to explain, lost
       in this habit of waiting,
walking on this stolen, sweat-stained
       bloody air
& you are everywhere
but I have to call you
       to be seen in the shape
of what I give to you daily.

Know I know I am not alone.
This is about a face inside a face
inside another & a single set of eyes
looking out into the world.
About a landscape.

Sweeping

This morning, in Fundeci
the breadman's basket weighed him
down & his call was a broken bird's.
This morning, the broom man came
at five a.m. crying *¡Escobas! ¡Escobas!* as if
he hadn't slept all night,
as if he had been crying *Sorrow! Murder!*
It is so many years before a war is over.

Yesterday, in Fundeci
a woman swept the front of her house,
hills reflected on the sweat
at the curve of her back,
and her boy, the boy
who dug up dead bullets from the swollen
earth of nearby yards, found one
he hammered into life.
It traveled between his eyes,
only blocks away from her.

This afternoon she sweeps
in long, steady strokes
as if she were crying
The heat! The sweltering heat!, meaning
to come up for air.

Nicaragua, 1991

Wild Animals on the Moon

— for Ivor Delve

> *Second rule of the road:*
> *any wound will stop*
> *bleeding if you press*
> *down hard enough.*
> — Audre Lorde, in *Shorelines*

A teacher, world traveler
rummages through notes one day.
        Decides the chatter of rain
inside the branches of a tree
        tells everything, is history
talking back:

The echo of bombs. Mindanao
        dusk. Helicopter
 blades cut sound, travel.
        A moon
red above the Philippines.

Averts the fell swoop
        of ammunition
by the Ferris wheel
        of a carnival in Morong.
        Stuck up top, drunk.

While Cambodian, Laotian
        Vietnamese
            refugees he teaches English to
        scatter beneath with ghosts
        like fire on their backs.
Later,
        he trains them on proper ways
            to interview for jobs
        in America

biting the inside
            of his mouth.
After the grass
            grows wild
  on former missile
            launching-pad land,
there is the chatter of rain
inside the branches
            of a tree.
Your history talking back.
Many moons above Morong
                  & Mindanao. A refugee
  who can't forget & you
  see it in his gaze
forever, counting wild
            animals on the moon
  on some late-night
            drunk. One, two, three,
            four-million-ever
growing,

            to the mad beat
  of a typewriter in the dark
  waiting to teach English
            in the morning —
  forget the way eyes
            glance up from the papers
  to breathe more easily
  not have to come back home.

This Breathless Minute

Our blood runs free forever before we ever
do. Do this, do that but our blood glides
smoothly the way we sometimes wish
we could — over concrete, past the screeching
wheels of patrol cars, stunning the whiteness
of emergency after emergency come
a little too late. I am sick
to breathlessness. My body's sick. I
got the cancer you get from the spell
spilled blood casts on you. Everywhere I look
blood brands a housefront, draws a line
of impermanence across a child's butterflied belly —
no growing down into her bones
before she gets that glimpse
of the bridge across, a bridge we think is sturdy
and will hold our walking. I am trying to stay
inside this country. I am trying very hard
to stay inside this country — today, this afternoon,
this breathless minute, but everybody's blood
is mixed into the blood that runs through here
and I can't tell my left foot
from my right hand.

Haiti

She reaches for her eyes
in street center, full view of the camera crews
as if cut glass had scraped
the eyelids — her face
gathered into an "o"
round as the snout of a gas mask,
stops there, apart from her body.
Her fingers curve
inward, arthritically,
one at a time.

No circles. No song.
The moon is bare white.
Other hands, like her own
grip their bellies
as if something greater than life
could rise up through
from the island floor
be crammed in them full
kicking and taking their air.

We watch them, watch her
flash across the t.v. screen
stay tuned for the car commercials
the new Caribbean vacation packages.
We return to work on time.

Behind the woman whose face is an "o"
a boat docks — weighed down with the dead
returned overnight in body bags better
than yesterday's clothes —
and she cannot move toward it.
There is nothing else to report.

Statement

The cop who tried to hustle
me between Nicoll Street & the open
August afternoon did not think
my garbanzo skin could be white
like the kinfolk do at Chico's
open air market, kinfolk at whose side
I choose strange roots by name,
pick out the ripest plantain,
the surest avocado.

In the open August afternoon
I was open like a child,
grip on a ten speed's handlebars
down the length of a city block

but the cop
who tried to hustle me perceived
my small body like a frail branch
one that invited to be cut
from the landscape.

When I did not
respond with my body
to the slowing speed of his car,
his motioning finger,
the roll of his tongue around his mouth,
he locked his eyes on mine,
called out "Latina! Aren't you?,"
demanding my address,
questioning
what I was doing in the neighborhood.

Leaving the patrol car,
his hand moved to handle the gun
in his holster the way a cock
is handled like a gun —

the screech of my brakes
stretching down the spine
of the empty street.

I would not go with him.
Would not leave to be
identified in a strange house
somewhere across town
for stealing goods
from neighbors' garages, making
off with the loot back of my bike.

I was not brave.
I fast-forwarded the backyard
and alleyway maze in my mind's eye,
thinking *runrunrun*,
willing to be shot for it.
I was firm, yelled
at the token trees to climb
out from their sidewalk shoes
and come witness. I believed God
was asleep in Hawaii
and would not wake to call me
from a payphone.

I was not intelligent, I claimed
having done nothing,
where nothing is still punishable
till a neighbor came,
threatened a witness.

Later, I could not make
an official complaint — you can't,
picked out in the street like that.
For weeks I was ashamed,
the way the raped are first ashamed
and silent.

Amber Hands

I am homesick in america
and it is always summertime,
that summer I am leaving
Puerto Rico, you, *abuela's*
tobacco-picking fingers
illustrating stories in the spiraling
afternoon light.

You, *abuelo* Juan, always
duro, fuerte —
that summer, at 89 years
jogging at dawn by the river,
riding your bicycle into market
for your *viandas*, me on the back.

Always *duro, fuerte*
and skeptical
of coming here, *siempre*
of truly finding america
but *siempre*
conmigo
and I, here, always with you.

You built my inheritance
with your amber hands, cautiously, alone —
leaf by aching leaf boiled
down for *purgante*,
medicine,
by each flower of *flamboyán* —
in a place where now
fastfood joints jam the outskirts
of rainforest, where neon ambition robs
the ancestral graves
of the home-spirit.

Nothing, *abuelo*
not the great indelible
million dollar dream,
the prime time news of disposable
contraptions to make life a clean-ass breeze,
could filter through the plantain
stain of my hands.

I am homesick,
summertime, that summer I am
leaving home without you, without *abuela*;
leaving behind
the basket of bean pods unshelled
on the rail of the veranda,
the dappled light on the empty hammock,
the song of wind in the canefields
pouring over the Dutch door
into your quiet wooden house,
that bike route into town along the river,
Rio Grande, I take to become grown up:
a young girl with a one way
ticket to cross *el charco*
because like you she was
dura, fuerte and a woman.

I draw the spirit of your life
to me, *abuelo*, past every highway.
I tip my straw hat the way
you taught me and know you feel me
as I do you, *presente*.
There is no distance.
There is no *charco*.

For Late Night Poems

i told you yesterday, done tell you
ten goddamn times you have to come
like horses galloping dreams
with muscle. Got to have
the staying power of hand to mouth
vibrations of verification, the truth
of rice & beans. Quit hiding on me
behind the leaf, behind the blade
when you're afraid
to speak, to be so goddamn human.
Risk your kayak
to blood river rapid fever
journeys, not pull your mouth away
from the stain of plátanos & caímito,
the quiver of wind in your wings,
hide from crows
in surreptitious superstitions
& get me so damn tired of you
scheming ways to climb my lips,
divulging your ego-tripping
way of tapping my sister's, brother's drum
with my notes turned steel.
i done tell you so goddamn enough
you're the cursed nicotine thickness
of my midnight throat,
that if you're gonna come
to take my milk from me,
you better do it in my sleep
if you cannot bare
the hands that yield to you down
to the bone marrow.

IV.

Secrets

They tore your pockets
into large whispering mouths,
backed up your dreams,
crawled under your mattress
and shook the bed at night.
They were the lead in your shoes,
a lost watch in threadbare dawns.
I woke with you and cried with you.
I watched you sleep under the broken
moonlight of the trees —
one eye keeping guard
as if the sky had eyes
and leaves could speak, roots cough
themselves out of the earth screaming.
You waited away the years
for all the if's that turned
loose doorknobs in the middle of the night
to burst into your hiding.

Personal History

When your history gets too big
to keep fitting in the wagon
you've been pulling all your life
your sleep is thin as water
you zigzag up hills
rely on a ladder to climb into your hammock
flush the toilet with a stick
pick tomatoes with a long steel hook
open beans up with a knife
cut the flowers in your garden with your pride.

There is no Spring like another Spring,
no lover like another come before,
and dreams, they all have a familiar sound
like a song on the radio,
a new pair of shoes,
a phone call in the middle of the night.

When your history gets too big
to keep fitting in the wagon
you've been pulling all your life
you leave your keys
where you meant never to go back,
remember what you wanted to forget —
a stranger on the street
selling songs for a dime,
like you his face, his eyes,
his song, his story —

because you are kin with all things now:
the man you kicked into the wall,
the car you crashed,
the food you cannot eat,
the whisper of countries
that open before you in the street,
the mechanical laughter behind the prime

time of your day, somebody else's dreams.
When your history gets that big
you walk backwards as you pull,
run after things that fall out on the street
forget exactly what it is you carry
in that wagon but live your life
as if you knew, always looking
for the sides of things that slope
down smoothly from a straight line across,
the memory that fits
so easily in your pocket.

Morela from Peru

At the Howard Johnson's on 42nd Street—

after the gay, gay Sicilian confessed
shyly in the corner about his previous marriage
to a Dominican woman
and later demanded I hear about
his knowledge of Arawak in the middle
of my poem about it at the bookstore,
before reading his own poem
about young gay men dead out
in the gutter with plastic bags over their heads
and old men getting laid in Grattsville;
after the frail woman on medication
whom I'd treated to coffee earlier
dotted the last lines of her poems
about shattered
institutionalist insomnia & "daddy rape"
with low vows while tearing
at a hole in her jeans;
and the young man flirting
with an icecube in his mouth
while reading his poem on open wombs
that bled in the middle of the night;
and the four-eyed android-dog poem inventor;
and the timid AIDS victim
who could only read his poetry
under the assumed
name of The Doorknob Sisters —

you could cut down my laughter
like a tree, had me say Boricua
one more time because you enjoyed
it in my poem, that word;
said I possessed
a rare gift of humor in my hands,

hands you examined like a woman does
a man's dozen roses, made me
touch them, admit they were beautiful,

made me lift my arms over my head
to remind their muscles to unlearn
the folded, remissive position
of centuries of women
and you
and your friends — all dancers —
stopped to look at my feet
because it was the first thing
you examined in people.

And I went on laughing Morela,
an awkward detour from the eager
warmth of your hands.
Hands that sought me
and the approval of your lover
who was there,
who could but encourage
you to be Morela,
Peruvian woman saved
from Pizarro's axes
coming to dance wildfire in New York City,
wanting to know had I a lover,
was he a man, and from somewhere
behind my woman's words
would I not approve of women lovers,
take one for myself? Take you?

I returned from Manhattan
and the reading with a tape of it
and your feet, for weeks, dancing out
the collective madness
of our lives in my mind's eye.

A Coquí in Nueva York

I am a loud mouth coquí
that broke out from the island
because the yanquis were
crowding the place, talking 'bout
chopping up trees in El Yunque — as if
paper products could feed
the eyes or fill the lungs — talking
'bout turning Loiza
into an open-air museum,
'bout eating broken English anthems
for breakfast at school
& how wonderful
& necessary it all was.
In the gallery
of their economic dreams
I sat by, shoving my song
deep into the fat briefcases
of their intentions
& sandwiched
between so much crap I knew
it would rot & make a stink
they'd have to tend to sometime.
All I wanted was to sing,
sing of my green onlyness.
I braved it to Nueva York with an attitude
I could sing where
I wanted what I wanted to.
I would invade the land of freedom with songs
that rotted into stinks
songs that drew people, made them move
toward the dance of action,
songs that composted
the garbage of nightmares
into fine, fine food.
I trained my song to live on air
years at a time, to leap

the tall buildings of frustration
and no-peace until I could smuggle it
back home & forth the back door way
& it multiply
& multiply
there & here.
And so I am alive today
& I call that a victory.
My song may be missing
a few fingers & its legs be bandaged up
but it's alive, loud, brave.

My Brother Pito

My voice, when I ache for his
is the steering
wheel of a car under my fingers
in wintertime
before the car warms up.

His voice,
a voice whose words I rummage
through like a dresser drawer
where everything falls in and away
and is bound
to show up somewhere sometime.

Voice of *naranja dulce* and
limón partido...
Voice of give and embrace.

Voice like train tracks
fade into the skyline,
into a fine nowhere I never
get to see long enough to
follow the wind.

Palm leaf, ripe mango skin voice,
he gives to me a joy
of spirit like coconut
water in dessert heat, enough
for me, enough to pass around.

For "S"

If a green leaf is no more alive to you
than your toe is without you
then go on about your life
flattening soda pop
cans for a pastime
leaning against the concrete
walls of shopping plazas
or gray corporate buildings waiting
on some cash to rain down
leaning against the soft side
of a woman trying hard to be gentle & alive
you can watch t.v.
tan in its technicolor splendor
though maybe
a toe's better off without you
sure it could feed something
sometime
or some new thing
shoot out from it like huckleberry
from a dead tree

Consuelo

I have been a bad girl, like my mother
taught me and her mother before her.
I have been all over my body with no
with narrow answers
to questions I've forgotten.
I've shaved my legs and brows clean
of the wild thing
in me I am defining today
to get through.

Consuelo, you have no name
in my neighborhood
no address.
Don't know where to find you
naked and pure
with tough love.
Where is the you in me
in the color of my eyes,
in the shape of my mouth
in the tint of the skin of my heart?
Where, Consuelo, is the food that feeds
you into a food for action?

I have been a bad, bad girl
like my mother taught me
and her mother before her.
I have draped men over my body
like foreign flags
whose national hymns I could not sing
for whom I hummed
and was solemn.
I have mistaken myself
for a mistaken identity.

It was written that I
look for you. The gauze
of your shadow

in the dawn dream
of waking over and over again
into strangeness
into the wrong body.

It can silence me so
looking for you beyond the trainyard
city, corner-bodega maze of my migrations that my tongue is a
lopped
off limb convulsing
its way closer to love without words.

I have mistaken myself
for whom I thought I could be
put away neatly
from she who was in every cell
all hunger, all passion.

I have been a bad, bad girl
like my mother taught me
and her mother before her--
shadow-lover, ass-kisser of fear
a courier for the bossman
of the caesuras in dreams
I knew not enough to play
let him sell to me
as the grave plots of silence.

May all those I love find you
for me, for every bad girl who dreamt
of your noon-time kiss
at the siesta of her faltering
prayers, groped in the dark
for a name to give you, Consuelo
in the every language of her woman self.

Lawns

the magnolia tree I've claimed in full
April bloom & come visit
is in someone else's yard, has a surname
that corresponds to a playpen
of a parcel & its owner
and I think that lawns
are a concept of colonialist
empires, that hedges symbolize
prisons beautified
fences you cannot not cross

like straps for oxen they tighten
around the back of the eyes
of your soul, wrap & bear weight
leave open sores to become
the landing strips of flies

I have turned organic fences
& frontyards in my dreams
over & over — a country-full
and know they become walls
against their will

rebel by growing every
which way every so often
in the middle of the dark
that only blades can trim
their constant disobedience

Up in the Air

Home is where I am,
within me.
— Alberto Sandoval,
"Puerto Rican Identity Up in the Air"

Now that I am a middle child
the sky is older
set farther back
the ground below swollen,
as if beneath a glass.

I live in the house
between ground and sky.
I am a middle child
and my *betweenness*
is audible.
It dyes the color of my speech,
glistens when I sweat
through the acrobatics of daily living.

I am a middle child,
and to live here
I have lived many deaths.
Death now has a home in me

and now that I can see
the Earth beneath my feet, it too is
an island.

NAOMI AYALA is a native of Puerto Rico. She has worked as an arts and education administrator, a coordinator of science programs, and is currently an education consultant, freelance writer, and teacher. She is Co-Chair of the Board of Directors of *Teaching for Change: Building Social Justice Starting in the Classroom,* and serves as the Mt. Pleasant Neighborhood Public Library's first Writer-in-Residence. In this capacity she founded *Punto Vivo*—a program that brings literary programming and educational resources to that neighborhood's community in Washington, DC.

photo © Desepe de Vargas

Ms. Ayala's poetry has appeared in numerous journals and anthologies in the U.S. and beyond—among them, *Callaloo, The Village Voice, The Caribbean Writer, The Massachusetts Review, Red River and Potomac Reviews, Hanging Loose* and *Terra Incognita.*

She is the recipient of the 2001 District of Columbia's Commission on the Arts and Humanities Larry Neal Writers Award for Poetry. In 2000 she received the *Dr. Martin Luther King, Jr. Legacy of Environmental Justice Award.* Her administration and community outreach work have earned Ms. Ayala Congressional recognition.

During a more than 1,000-mile hike of the Appalachian Trail in the spring of 2000, Ms. Ayala walked from Springer Mountain in Georgia to Wingdale, New York. She values the outdoors and celebrates the sacred connection between the individual and the earth.

She is currently at work on a second book of poetry and a translation of Gioconda Belli's poetry.

CURBSTONE PRESS, INC.

is a nonprofit publishing house dedicated to literature that reflects a commitment to social change, with an emphasis on contemporary writing from Latino, Latin American and Vietnamese cultures. Curbstone presents writers who give voice to the unheard in a language that goes beyond denunciation to celebrate, honor and teach. Curbstone builds bridges between its writers and the public – from inner-city to rural areas, colleges to community centers, children to adults. Curbstone seeks out the highest aesthetic expression of the dedication to human rights and intercultural understanding: poetry, testimonies, novels, stories, and children's books.

This mission requires more than just producing books. It requires ensuring that as many people as possible learn about these books and read them. To achieve this, a large portion of Curbstone's schedule is dedicated to arranging tours and programs for its authors, working with public school and university teachers to enrich curricula, reaching out to underserved audiences by donating books and conducting readings and community programs, and promoting discussion in the media. It is only through these combined efforts that literature can truly make a difference.

Curbstone Press, like all nonprofit presses, depends on the support of individuals, foundations, and government agencies to bring you, the reader, works of literary merit and social significance which might not find a place in profit-driven publishing channels, and to bring the authors and their books into communities across the country. Our sincere thanks to the many individuals, foundations, and government agencies who have supported this endeavor: Connecticut Commission on the Arts, Connecticut Humanities Council, Eastern CT Community Foundation, Fisher Foundation, Greater Hartford Arts Council, Hartford Courant Foundation, J. M. Kaplan Fund, Lamb Family Foundation, Lannan Foundation, John D. and Catherine T. MacArthur Foundation, National Endowment for the Arts, Open Society Institute, Puffin Foundation, United Way, and the Woodrow Wilson National Fellowship Foundation.

Please help to support Curbstone's efforts to present the diverse voices and views that make our culture richer. Tax-deductible donations can be made by check or credit card to:
Curbstone Press, 321 Jackson Street, Willimantic, CT 06226
phone: (860) 423-5110   fax: (860) 423-9242
www.curbstone.org

IF YOU WOULD LIKE TO BE A MAJOR SPONSOR OF A
CURBSTONE BOOK, PLEASE CONTACT US.